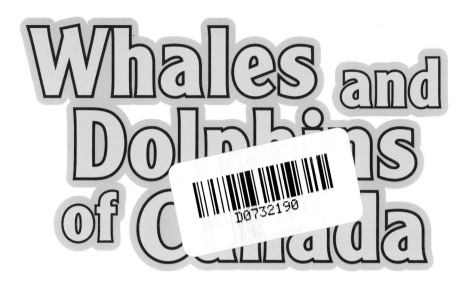

Whales and Dolphins of Canada

Einstein Sisters

KidsWorld

About Whales & Dolphins

Whales and dolphins are very intelligent. Some scientists think that these mammals are as smart as humans.

A group of whales or dolphins is called a pod.

Tail Stock

Fluke

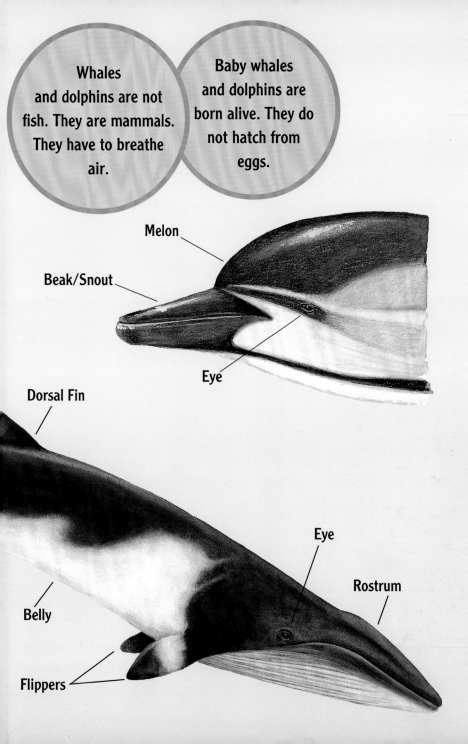

Whales and dolphins are not fish. They are mammals. They have to breathe air.

Baby whales and dolphins are born alive. They do not hatch from eggs.

Melon

Beak/Snout

Eye

Dorsal Fin

Belly

Flippers

Eye

Rostrum

Whales & Dolphins Are Different

Many whales
have two blowholes,
but some have only one.
Dolphins always
have only one
blowhole.

These dolphins are
called whales, but they're not:
Orca (sometimes called Killer Whale)
Pygmy Killer Whale
False Killer Whale
Long-finned Pilot Whale
Short-finned Pilot Whale

The biggest whales have baleen, but some whales have teeth. All dolphins have teeth.

Whales have some hair on their bodies. Dolphins don't have any hair.

Blue whale

Bottlenose dolphin

Whales are usually bigger than dolphins (but not always).

Whales often have bumpy skin and barnacles. Dolphins have very smooth skin.

Blowholes & Blows

Whales and dolphins have lungs like we do, but their lungs are much larger.

Humans breathe automatically, but whales and dolphins must decide when to breathe.

Paired blowholes of baleen whale

Whales and dolphins breathe air through blowholes at the top of their heads. A blowhole is kind of like your nose.

Whales usually sleep on the surface of the water. Dolphins can stay underwater because they sleep with half their brain at a time. The other half stays awake so the dolphin can come to the surface to breathe.

Whales and dolphins can't sneeze.

The blowhole closes when the whale or dolphin dives.

Single blowhole of dolphin

Whales can hold their breath for a really long time. The record is a sperm whale that stayed underwater for 2 hours and 18 minutes.

Baleen & Teeth

Bowhead whale baleen

Minke whale baleen

Baleen whales eat very small sea creatures called krill. Krill are like tiny shrimp. These whales also eat plankton. Plankton are tiny plants and animals that live in the ocean.

Some whales eat about one tonne (1000 kg) of food each day. That's the same as a large car weighs.

Toothed whales and dolphins are hunters. They eat fish, squid, crabs, sea stars and other ocean creatures. They usually swallow their prey whole.

Some whales and dolphins have teeth, but the biggest whales have "baleen."

Baleen is like a big strainer. The whale opens its mouth and swallows a lot of water. The water flows through the baleen, and the baleen traps small creatures that the whale eats.

Baleen is made out of keratin. Your fingernails and hair are also made out of keratin.

Orca teeth

Echolocation

Dolphins and toothed whales, such as belugas, narwhals, sperm whales and beaked whales, use echolocation to find food. Bats and some birds also use echolocation.

Echolocation helps whales and dolphins find food in the dark or in murky water.

To use echolocation, a whale or dolphin makes high-pitched sounds. Then it listens to how the sounds bounce off nearby objects.

Whales and dolphins also use echolocation for navigation. It tells them what is in the water around them.

Why Do Whales Migrate?

Whales migrate to eat, mate and give birth to baby whales, called "calves."

The krill that baleen whales eat live in cold water, so the whales spend the summer in northern oceans eating.

The mother whales swim from cold northern oceans to warm southern oceans to have their calves. When calves are born, they don't have any body fat, so they must be born in warm water.

Some whales make long migrations. Grey whales and humpback whales make the longest migrations.

Whale Migration

Grey whales

Grey whales migrate from summer feeding grounds in the north Pacific Ocean to winter breeding grounds off the coast of Mexico. They return north again in spring.

Grey whales make the longest migration of any mammal on Earth. It's a round trip of about 20,000 kilometres.

Humpback whales

The humpback whale's migration is a round trip of about 10,000 kilometres.

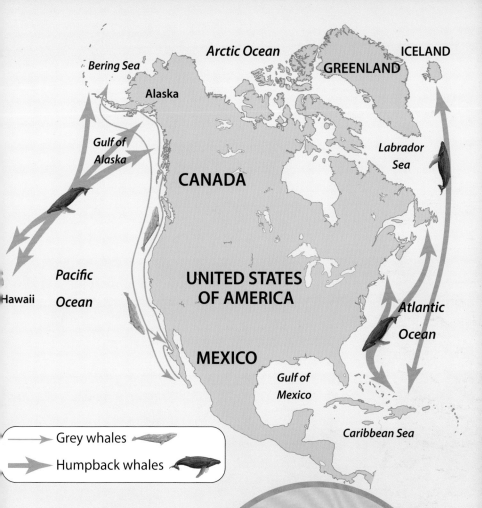

Arctic Ocean

ICELAND

Bering Sea

GREENLAND

Alaska

Gulf of
Alaska

Labrador
Sea

CANADA

Pacific

UNITED STATES
OF AMERICA

Atlantic

Hawaii

Ocean

Ocean

MEXICO

Gulf of
Mexico

Caribbean Sea

Grey whales

Humpback whales

A pod of
humpbacks travels
at about 5 to 11 kilometres
per hour and makes very
few stops.

In summer,
humpback whales live in
the northern Pacific and Atlantic
Oceans. In winter, humpbacks in the
Pacific Ocean migrate to waters
near Hawaii. Humpbacks in the
Atlantic Ocean migrate to
the Caribbean.

Breach: A whale breaches when it rises out of the water and splashes back in. Dolphins sometimes do a high leap and even a somersault when they breach.

Log: Whales log on the surface of the water so they can rest. They can't sleep underwater because they need to breathe. When whales log together, they always face the same direction.

Lob-tail: A lob-tail is when a whale slaps its tail flukes on the water, but its body stays under the water.

Flipper-slap: Whales and dolphins sometimes roll to one side and slap a flipper on the water.

Bow-ride: Dolphins and small whales sometimes "surf" on the wave in front of a boat. The wave pushes the animals along.

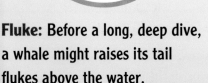

Fluke: Before a long, deep dive, a whale might raises its tail flukes above the water.

Spy-hop: When a whale spy-hops, it raises just its head out of the water to see what's around it.

Grey Whale

Dive Sequence

WHERE FOUND: In the northern Pacific Ocean.
LENGTH: 14 metres
WEIGHT: 32,000 kilograms

Grey whales spend the summer in the Arctic. Then they migrate south to warm waters off Mexico, where they spend the winter.

Grey whales eat tiny creatures called amphipods. Amphipods are like little shrimp.

Grey whales don't have a dorsal fin. They have a ridge of small bumps called "knuckles" along their back.

Blow

Minke Whale

Minke whales spend less time on the surface than other whales. They come up to take a quick breath, then dive again.

A minke whale can hold its breath for 25 minutes.

Minke whales spend the summer in cold Arctic waters. In winter, they swim south to warmer oceans.

Dive Sequence

WHERE FOUND: **In every ocean in the world.**
LENGTH: **8 metres**
WEIGHT: **10,000 kilograms**

These whales usually swim alone or in small groups of four to six. Minke whales can live for up to 60 years.

Blow

Sei Whale

This whale makes very loud, low-pitched sounds. Sei whales can live for 65 years.

Dive Sequence

The sei whale is the third largest whale in the world. Only the blue whale and the fin whale are bigger.

The sei whale is one of the fastest whales.

Blow

Blue Whale

Dive Sequence

WHERE FOUND: In every ocean in the world.
LENGTH: 26 metres
WEIGHT: 109,000 kilograms

The blue whale is the largest creature on Earth. It is also the loudest. Blue whales are very rare.

This whale's tongue weighs 2700 kilograms. That's about the same as two cars!

A blue whale can't swallow anything larger than a beach ball. It eats tiny, shrimp-like creatures called "krill."

Blow

Fin Whale

Even though it is very big, this whale can jump completely out of the water.

The fin whale has a ridge along its back. Its nickname is "razorback."

The lower jaw is black on the left side and white on the right side.

A fin whale can live for almost 100 years.

Dive Sequence

WHERE FOUND: In every ocean in the world. It is more common in the Southern Hemisphere.
LENGTH: 21 metres
WEIGHT: 73,000 kilograms

The fin whale is the second largest whale in the world. Only the blue whale is bigger.

Blow

Humpback Whale

Dive Sequence

These whales are curious and will come close to boats.

Humpback whales have very long flippers.

These whales sing long, complicated songs. They use these songs to communicate with other humpbacks.

Humpbacks like to breach. They also slap their flippers on the water.

Humpback whales only eat when they are in the Arctic in summer. In the winter, they migrate up to 25,000 kilometres to warm oceans to mate and give birth to their calves.

Blow

Northern Right Whale

It is called the right whale because long ago, it was the "right" whale to hunt. Now it is illegal to kill this whale.

Southern right whales live in the Southern Hemisphere.

These whales are playful and curious. They sometimes lift or bump boats for fun.

The northern right whale is the slowest whale.

Dive Sequence

WHERE FOUND: In cold oceans in the Northern Hemisphere.
LENGTH: 14 metres
WEIGHT: 54,000 kilograms

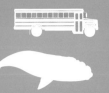

Blow

Bowhead Whale

This whale has a very large skull. The skull takes up about one-third of its body. The bowhead whale's large head allows it to break through thick ice.

Dive Sequence

Bowhead whales can live for 200 years.

This whale swims slowly. It usually travels alone or in small pods with up to six members.

Blow

Beluga

Belugas
have a thick layer
of fat that keeps them
warm in the icy water.
This fat is called
"blubber."

WHERE FOUND: In Arctic seas.
LENGTH: 4 metres
WEIGHT: 820 kilograms

Belugas can make many different sounds. Some people call them "sea canaries."

The beluga is the only whale that can swim backwards.

Baby belugas are grey. They turn white as they get older.

The beluga the only whale that can move its head from side to side and up and down.

Narwhal

These whales travel in pods of 15 to 20. They can live to be 50 years old.

Narwhals
eat fish, squid
and shrimp.

The narwhal is known as the "unicorn of the sea."

The narwhal's "tusk" is a really long tooth. Usually only the male narwhals have a tusk. The tusk always spirals to the left.

Narwhals are related to belugas.

Sperm Whale

Dive Sequence

WHERE FOUND: All the oceans of the world.
LENGTH: 15 metres
WEIGHT: 32,000 kilograms

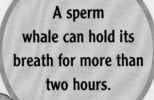

> A sperm whale can hold its breath for more than two hours.

The whale's head is filled with oil called "spermaceti," which is how the whale got its name. The oil helps the whale float or sink.

The sperm whale is one of the deepest diving whales. Only Cuvier's beaked whale can dive deeper.

Sperm whales eat mostly giant squid.

Blow

Cuvier's Beaked Whale

There are 20 kinds of beaked whales. Beaked whales have a long snout, or "beak."

It is difficult for scientists to study these whales because they like deep water and don't come close to shore.

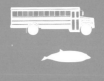

Beaked whales have very small dorsal fins and small, rounded flippers.

Cuvier's beaked whale can dive deeper and stay under water longer than any other whale. One of these whales dove to nearly 3000 metres.

Bottlenose Dolphin

Bottlenose dolphins are one of the most common kinds of dolphins. They are curious and friendly. They often come close to people.

This dolphin is one of the most intelligent animals. It has a very large brain.

Bottlenose dolphins swim to the surface two or three times a minute to breathe.

These dolphins "talk" to each other using squeaks and whistles.

If a dolphin is hurt, other members of the pod will help it surface to breathe.

Saddleback Dolphins

There are at least 20 kinds of saddleback dolphins. Most of them look almost the same.

Saddleback dolphins make many different sounds, including clicking, squeaking and whistling.

If these dolphins are startled, they gather together for safety.

WHERE FOUND: In warm oceans around the world. In Canada, they occur off the west coast of Vancouver Island.

LENGTH: 2 metres   WEIGHT: 77 kilograms

Saddleback dolphins hunt in pods. They eat mostly small fish.

Pacific White-sided Dolphin

These dolphins are curious and playful. They like to entertain people on boats.

Pacific white-sided dolphins sometimes tease humpback whales and orcas. The whales get fed up and dive to escape.

These dolphins have a very good sense of touch. They can feel small changes in pressure in the water around them.

WHERE FOUND: Only in the northern Pacific Ocean.
LENGTH: 2.1 metres
WEIGHT: 95 kilograms

Pacific white-sided dolphins sometimes gather in groups of 1000 or more.

Atlantic White-sided Dolphin

All dolphins have good eyesight both in and out of the water.

Atlantic white-sided dolphins are very social and playful. They like to lob-tail and breach.

These dolphins swim in pods of about 60. They often swim with humpback whales, fin whales, white-beaked dolphins and long-finned pilot whales.

WHERE FOUND: Only in the northern
Atlantic Ocean.
LENGTH: 2.4 metres
WEIGHT: 200 kilograms

Atlantic
white-sided dolphins
eat small fish and
squid.

White-beaked Dolphin

These dolphins like to bow-ride, so they often swim near boats. They also like to breach.

White-beaked dolphins eat fish. They also eat squid and crabs. Fishermen sometimes call these dolphins "squid hounds."

These dolphins hunt in groups. They "talk" to each other using whistles, tail slaps and leaps.

WHERE FOUND: Only in the northern
Atlantic Ocean.
LENGTH: 2.7 metres
WEIGHT: 220 kilograms

Risso's Dolphin

These dolphins don't like very cold water. They swim in deep water and don't come close to shore.

Risso's dolphins are black, but they often have so many scars that they look almost white.

These dolphins eat mostly squid.

These dolphins travel in pods of up to 30. They sometimes form pods with other kinds of dolphins.

False Killer Whale

WHERE FOUND: In warm oceans around the world.
In Canada, it occurs along the BC coast.
LENGTH: 5.2 metres
WEIGHT: 1500 kilograms

The false killer whale is not a whale at all. It is the third largest dolphin in the world.

False killer whales sometimes mate with bottlenose dolphins. Their offspring are called "wolphins."

These dolphins eat squid and fish.

False killer whales can live for more than 60 years.

Long-finned Pilot Whale

The long-finned pilot whale is a kind of dolphin. It is related to the short-finned pilot whale but has longer flippers.

The white patch on this dolphin's belly looks like an anchor.

Long-finned pilot whales are very active and like to spy-hop and lob-tail.

These dolphins are very social and like to swim in large pods. A long-finned pilot whale may stay with the same pod for its whole life.

Orca

Dive Sequence

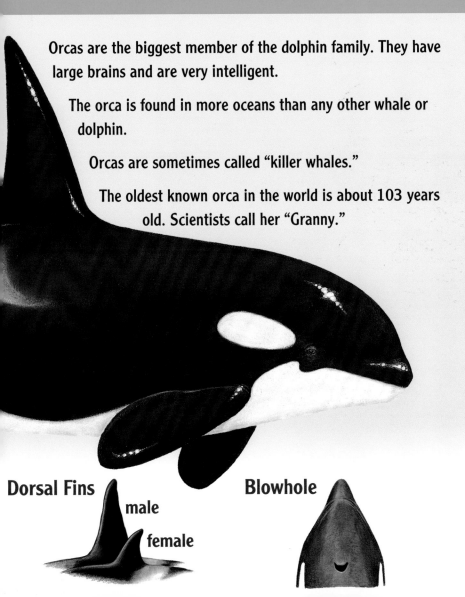

WHERE FOUND: In oceans around the world.
LENGTH: 8.5 metres
WEIGHT: 6800 kilograms

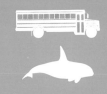

Orcas are the biggest member of the dolphin family. They have large brains and are very intelligent.

The orca is found in more oceans than any other whale or dolphin.

Orcas are sometimes called "killer whales."

The oldest known orca in the world is about 103 years old. Scientists call her "Granny."

Dorsal Fins

male

female

Blowhole

Harbour Porpoise

Porpoises
are similar to dolphins
but they have rounded
heads and no
beak.

WHERE FOUND: Near the coast in northern
oceans around the world.
LENGTH: 1.5 metres
WEIGHT: 60 kilograms

This porpoise swims in shallow waters along coastlines.

Harbour porpoises live in small pods of two to five.

When the porpoise comes to the surface, it makes a sneezing
sound. Some people call it "puffing porpoise."

Dall's Porpoise

Dall's porpoise is the largest member of the porpoise family.

This porpoise is curious and will come close to boats. It is a very fast swimmer.

Dall's porpoise looks like a baby orca.

© 2014 KidsWorld Books

First printed in 2014 10 9 8 7 6 5 4 3 2

Printed in China

The Publisher: KidsWorld Books

Library and Archives Canada Cataloguing in Publication

Whales & dolphins of Canada / Einstein Sisters.

ISBN 978-0-9938401-5-9 (pbk.)

1. Whales—Canada—Juvenile literature. 2. Dolphins—Canada—Juvenile literature. I. Einstein Sisters II. Title: Whales and dolphins of Canada.

QL737.C4W44 2014   j599.50971   C2014-903892-5

Cover Images: Front cover: bottlenose dolphin, federicoriz / Thinkstock. *Back cover:* humpback whale, Jim Tierney / Thinkstock; beluga, Fuse / Thinkstock.
Photo Credits: Andreas Tille / Flickr, 51; David B. Fleetham / Visuals Unlimited, 34; Debra McGuire / Thinkstock, 42; Eric Stoops / Corel Corporation, 21, 24, 38, 47, 62; François Gohier / ardea.com, 49; Jim Tierney / Thinkstock, 28; Jovana Milanko, 12–13; Ken Balcomb, 18, 60; Marty Snyderman / Visuals Unlimited, 31; NOAA Photo Library, 22, 33, 36, 45, 56; Øystein Paulsen, 8; rjones0856 / Flickr, 54; Silfox / Thinkstock, 27; Terry Parker, 58.
Illustrations: Ian Sheldon
Map: Volker Bodegom

We acknowledge the financial support of the Government of Canada through the Canada Book Fund (CBF) for our publishing activities.

Canadian   Patrimoine
Heritage   canadien

PC: 27